Love in a Time of Climate Change

poems by

Cindy Ellen Hill

Finishing Line Press
Georgetown, Kentucky

Love in a Time
of Climate Change

Copyright © 2025 by Cindy Ellen Hill
ISBN 979-8-89990-111-9 First Edition
All rights reserved under International and Pan-American Copyright Conventions. No part of this book may be reproduced in any manner whatsoever without written permission from the publisher, except in the case of brief quotations embodied in critical articles and reviews.

ACKNOWLEDGMENTS

My heartfelt thanks to all my poetry community: my Monday poetry collaborators Gail Schulte and Elizabeth Drewry Beck; my Vermont literary companions, particularly Buffy Aakaash and Dan Close for their keen eyes and editorial advice; my poetry quartet colleagues Marshall Witten, Richard Cuyler and Ann Cooper; and all my friends at the weekly Otter Creek Poets workshop, including our fearless leader of over twenty years, David Weinstock. Thanks also to artist Stein Kåre Nygård of Ålesund, Norway, for allowing me to use his painting Gylden Reise (Golden Journey) as the cover, perfectly capturing the fragility of relationships as we walk together into an uncertain future.

Gratitude to the publishers who previously presented works contained in this volume:

"Days of Man" appeared in *Wild Earth Magazine*, Fall 1991.
"Slipping" appeared in *Maps and Voyages Anthology*, Otter Creek Poets, 2004.
"Silver Solstice" appeared in Susan Jeft's Vermont-syndicated Poetry Matters column, December 2020, and in *Wild Earth*, Antrim Press 2022.
"Landscape: Cliffs Above the Sea" and "Climate Fire" appeared in *Wild Earth*, Antrim Press 2022.
"Turtle of the World" appeared in *Shadowplay*, May 2023.
"Traveler" and "Night Vision" appeared in *VerseVirtual*, July 2023.
"Which Side Are You On" and "Gambling" appeared in *MacQueen's Quinterly*, August 2023.
"Common" comprised part of a collaborative poem by the same name that appeared in *La Piccioletta Barca*, October 2023.
"Anthropomancy" appeared in *Ponder Review*, Autumn 2023.
"Hopeless Beauty", "Home Garden" and "Who Am I After This" appeared in *Stray Words Magazine*, 2024.
"Wandering Sorrow" appeared in the *Poem City* exhibit, Montpelier Vermont, April 2024.
"Walnut Bowl" appeared in *Bric-a-Brac*, Summer 2024.
"Blue Mother Writes to Carlo Rovelli About Reality" was published under a different title in *No Country*, June 26, 2024
"The Nettle Shirt" appeared in *Plant Human Quarterly*, Autumn Equinox 2025

Publisher: Leah Huete de Maines
Editor: Christen Kincaid
Cover Art: Stein Kåre Nygård, Gylden Reise (Golden Journey), oil on canvas
Author Photo: Kristy Dooley
Cover Design: Elizabeth Maines McCleavy

Order online: www.finishinglinepress.com
also available on amazon.com

Author inquiries and mail orders:
Finishing Line Press
PO Box 1626
Georgetown, Kentucky 40324
USA

Contents

Spring
- The Break-Up ... 2
- March Snowfall (Spring Equinox) ... 3
- Sunday, Silver Lake ... 4
- Behind Us Like The Winter ... 5
- Tides ... 6
- Blue Mother ... 7
- Off The Abbey Pond Trail ... 8
- Banking On A Change Of Season ... 9
- Liberty NY 1977 ... 10
- Cascades ... 11
- April Fields ... 12
- Spring Fling ... 13
- Gone To Seed ... 14
- Hopeless Beauty ... 15
- Which Side Are You On ... 16
- The Common ... 17

Summer
- Dooryard In June ... 20
- Slipping ... 21
- Wandering Sorrow ... 22
- Shalimar Gardens ... 23
- A Neighbor Mows His Lawn ... 24
- The Nettle Shirt ... 25
- Blueberries ... 26
- Home Garden ... 27
- Depths ... 28
- Blue Mother Goes Wading ... 29
- Last Night ... 30
- Photosynthesis ... 31
- Turtle Of The World ... 32
- Days Of Man ... 33

A Middle-Aged Woman's Crush In Ten Sonnets
- 1: Meeting ... 36
- 2: The First Eight Hours ... 37
- 3: Second Meeting ... 38
- 4: Feeling Foolish ... 39

  5: Stasis 40
  6: Diffusion 41
  7: Today I Deleted Your Emails 42
  8: Who Am I After This? 43
  9: Fly Agaric 44
  10: Hundred-Year Storm 45

Autumn
  We Needed The Rain 48
  Culvert 49
  A House Left Empty 50
  Anthropomancy 51
  Expectation 53
  Blue Mother Has Had Enough Of Progress 54
  The Solid House 55
  Traveler 56
  Gambling 57
  Nature Morte 58
  Blue Mother Talks With Her Daughter 59
  Climate Fire 60
  Flower And Book 61
  Standing In Rain 62

Winter
  Stick Season 64
  Night Vision 65
  Love Waiting 66
  Silver Solstice 67
  Amtrak Ethan Allen Line In February 68
  Boundaries 69
  Walnut Bowl 70
  Frozen Pipes: A Love Sonnet 71
  Anxiety (And I Become A Pearl) 72
  Blue Mother Sits At Her She-Shed In Norway, Remembering
    The Ice Age 73
  Closing Up The Garden, Vermont In December 74
  In The Grey Light Of A Winter Afternoon 75
  Landscape: Cliffs Above The Sea 76
  Blue Mother Writes To Carlo Rovelli About Reality 77
  Melting (Love In A Time Of Climate Change) 79

in memory of my grandmother

Dorothy Evelyn Fowler

*who loved a good romance story
and all the pretty flowers*

i miss you

Spring

Spring has returned. The Earth is like a child that knows poems.

—Rainer Maria Rilke

The break-up

It came earlier each year, then not at all:
the break-up of ice on the White River.
The long-forgotten song of water rushing
over frozen plates where we had walked
just days before as streams of bubbles crawled
beneath the smooth white surface like rapture—
pulsing, unreachable. When the pressure
became too great to carry, the ice called
out in grief and pain. It groaned and strained
against the whole wide world which longed for spring.
Ground shook when winter shattered. Blue floes launched
skyward, soared like breaching whales. Slurry rained
down as we watched from the old iron bridge,
each leaning out, not knowing what we'd lost.

March snowfall (Spring equinox)

Grey mist over mountain snow.
Grey sky over grey mist.
Crowflight startles a white branch.
Small among small cascades.

Wet, erratic dreamlight falls
in dense walls of grey fog
between the limbs of spring-black trees
tracing winter's last wave

on edges of cold white foam;
slides under forest floor,
retreats in black seas of time,
birthnight of the season.

Beside the late-night burning hearth,
I dream within the one dark dream,
the white crowdream of winter's end,
springtime everblooms of passion:

> Red buds swell on thin grey branches.
> New white lambs in a red barn.
> Lifeblood of all born, creation
> stirs in mist-silver cups of dawn.

Sunday, Silver Lake

Seven white oak acorn caps
beneath an old field pine.

The body of the lake rises
yearning to be free of her shores.

A strong southeasterly wind obliges her desires,
but only for a time,
and only on the surface.

Drop by drop she flies on stinging wings.
All eyes cast downward to avoid
the salty tears she brings, unaware,

unintending,
as the tops of the old field pines
bend, threatening to snap, then
disappear inside a lake-filled sky.

Behind us like the winter

> *"Be in advance of all parting, as though it were behind you like the winter that is just going."*
> —Rilke, Sonnets to Orpheus, 2.13

Winter is behind us now, forever.
We have burned ice out of the heart of God
the way incense consumes the oxygen
inside sacred space, inviting visions

to arise where air wavers, where solid ground
gives way to eternal pixelations.
And who can breathe inside that kind of fire?
Not us. No, we are long gone from ourselves,

looking backward like bees flown from the hive
to see our own image in every cell,
marveling at the mountain of our wealth,
rubbing our hands around digital hearths,
remarking that it's got hotter than hell,
waiting patiently in the self-check-out line.

Tides

Each spring they dredge the sand
out of the inlet at Wildwood Crest,
and haul it to North Wildwood
to fill the beaches washed away
by winter storms.

Each morning a crew nearly one hundred
strong and wearing yellow vests
walks with bags and pointed sticks
to clear the beaches of trash dropped there
the day before.

Each hour the woman tending the public restroom
sweeps the grit that has been blown
into the stalls back out onto the boardwalk
where it falls between the boards
into the dark dune shade below.

Each minute someone shoos away a gull
dive-bombing for a pizza crust, then
smooths lotion over sunburned skin
cells that have already begun
their lethal divide.

Blue Mother

Blue Mother   shake off your rattlesnake
hills for the famine is   coming and
these are the   dreams we will need
for the   harvest tomorrow.

Blue Mother   put on your party dress
dance through the streets of New
York and Chicago unraveling
your ruffled hem on our ragged
uncertainty. Famine is   coming and
these are the   fields that we
cannot afford
to leave fallow.

Dream Mother   waken your oat-laden
mice. Set them gnawing the ragged
foundations of our unlived   unalive
plastic foam   poisonous lives.
If they gnaw through the   moorings
now while we are   sleeping
they might solve things   once
and for all.

Noble Mice   chew through those
strong ropes that   tether our dreams
to the concrete and parcel lines
quarterly profit   reports because
we are the famine that's coming
with carving knives.

Fill our dirigible dreams
with the seeds   of some world
lush and green, with rich grain
and tall trees and the chatter
of otters   or there will not be
a tomorrow.

Off the Abbey Pond Trail

forest soul emerges after rain

long slow dance of dying limb
and roots entwined in webs of pale
white mycorrhizal lace

a bead of silver-green rolls off a leaf

above, mosquitos whine through their
abbreviated lives

looks can be deceiving
but the red ones are inevitably
poisonous

Banking on a change of season

What if I wove a wide pinstripe
in woolen thread, in twill sett,
scribbled along margins of a menu
by brown riverbanks that underflow
a flitting mayfly banquet set
for rising stripe and thrashing flash
and sparkling pins of light
like coins in summer fountains
effervescence bet the bank on quiet
elegance, hand-picked and softly rolled
lapels, sage-buttered fins
and tail sweet-roasted over
charcoal embers earthen-banked,
wrapped in parchment tied and
plaited in new green grass stems
where blue river courses through
bright plates laid out for luncheon
on a penny-colored blanket
hand-basted with a hint it might be
lined with chartreuse silk.

Liberty NY 1977
    to Kim Schindler

while the men all
        fished the Beaverkill
we found a bobcat cave
            dug in the side of a ravine,
                  rank with flies
and full of broken bones

whenever I would cast,
        my fly would tangle
                in an overhanging tree limb,
                        hand-tied feathers yearning
to return to leaf and sky

        get down from there,
your father yelled
as our legs dangled
over the lodge eaves,
ragged shingles slick
with moss and pine
        that's the way to make angels

we smoked our cigarettes
        and flung the spent butts
spinning through
        the effervescent balsam

then slipped, hang-dog,
        between dark paneling
        and wine-thick Persian rugs,
brass racks of crystal tumblers,
        oil-on-board hounds and horses,
            and padded past
the hovering heads
of deer long dead
whose bright black eyes
still glittered

Cascades

There was you and there was me. A fish moved
upstream, undulating in a speckled
dream beneath a surface, sunlight-spackled,
where leaf-points dangled. My touch was reproved
by your rough woolen side glance. No bell chime
from distant town could reach us here. Bees drown
among the river stones. You gently set one down
to dry while whispering,
                        Am I in time?
I shake my head. No, that was long ago,
before mayflies died out. Hollow knotweed
palisades the banks. Rush and roar, worn stones
will break, tumble and clatter. Only flow
endures. Movement, not matter. This alone
cascades through mossy glades, a slender reed.

April fields

Luck of a fish, to be caught inside pieces of sky
mirrored in shallow lakes skimming the low-lying fields.
Snow melt and spring rain has lifted the brown trout and eels
over the riverbanks, passing the fiddleheads by,
on through the willows, o'er timothy, clover and rye,
into rough furrows where recently ravens had dined,
gleaning old corn between tiny round tunnels that wind
under the ground where reflections of buzzards now fly.

Trout season opens, but rivers are churning with mud,
weight of the world dragging mountains down into the vales.
Tender green shoots bring no solace to floundering tails
caught in the breathtaking force of a warm April flood.
Field mouse and fish, both meet their mortal end there;
one drowning in water, the other one drowning in air.

Spring fling

She pulled my silver flattery
        across her breast
        laid back to rest
and said I was the best
        the best
        the best of all the daffodils
in a whole sea of daffodils
blossoming gold on sloping hills
the brightest yellow daffodil
to brighten her jonquility
amid fresh green tranquility—
forget-me-nots in beds of blue
and bees that buzzed
and birds that flew—
and then the heavy tulips grew
and when the late, dark lilacs bloomed
they heralded my withered doom
and when the roses raised their heads
I knew her love for me was dead.

I heap on roses all the blame
for putting spring's fleet joy to shame.

Gone to seed

We do not cut down the back
until forget-me-nots
have gone to seed.

Over the years, the blue has
sported white, and tall
among them rise spires of
purple cranesbill, wild
lettuce and silver dollar.

There some lamium.
And there some dutchman's breeches
and some bleeding hearts.

My neighbor mows his lawn
and casts a rueful eye this way.

I think if we were not home
all the color in the world
would fall to his
incessant spinning blade.

Hopeless beauty

> *"...the hopelessness. Whatever hope is yours,*
> *was my life also; I went hunting wild*
> *After the wildest beauty in the world"*
> —Wilfred Owen, Strange Meeting

On thin, folded blankets, the hopelessness
of my dreams waits in a blue box. Such hope

as lies inside its wooden walls is yours
along with all the dust there ever was.

No surprise there, this containment of my
rumpled demeanor, my grey-flannel life,

my absence. But tell the truth: You also
knew I'd take myself wherever I went.

And how I went—through mossy greenwood, hunting
into the thick-wet wide-striped windy wild.

You weren't the first illusion I'd chased after,
nor the swiftest white hart, nor the wildest.

Though I confess you're still a rare beauty,
like spring-gold daffodils shattered,
                              scattered newly in the world.

Which Side Are You On
in memoriam Daniel Ellsberg 1931-2023
after Ted Berrigan 1934-1983

Daniel Ellsberg died while I was driving
among clouds. Where do demons go to hide
our thoughts from all the forces that conspire
past a square white church in a flooded field,
now that our own front doors cannot conceal
its ragged slate roof on its short white spire
punctuating one bare patch of blue sky
to turn us into circuit boards who buy.
They hardly bother. They just stroll inside,
shining; objective anything but clear.
I think the point is for us to consume
everything without question. Nothing blooms.
They pop open your eyes, count the cold beer
left in your fridge and order you some more
on credit cards. Oh, this is still a war
but no one recalls the smell of newsprint.
Ink smeared our fingers. Pixels blind our mind.

The Common

When someone says, "the safety of the nest"
no one on earth need ask what those words mean.
We hold that globe of reference in our dreams
or in the soft flesh of a lover's breast.

Crossing Boston Common in a deluge,
a silent old man appeared, suddenly,
through dim grey sheets of rain. He shielded me
with his umbrella, a gift of refuge.

There comes a time to step outside, to fly
and fall to certain death on the sidewalk.
Between faltering beats of wings one cry
escapes all living throats, a common call:

"I first slept in the fullness of a round
embrace, and ever since have sought
that downy bed. Great battles I have fought
alone, but it is nowhere to be found."

Summer

I almost wish we were butterflies and liv'd but three summer days...

—John Keats

Dooryard in June

A man walks from the darkness of the barn
into white sun. His t-shirt hangs untucked,
his khaki pants bloused carelessly above
tall mud-streaked boots.
                                        Beyond, a flock of gulls
wheels above the plowed part of the field.
His forearms flex, his fingers tightly furled
around the bolt needed to fix the tractor.

Inside the quiet house an unborn child
turns, dreaming not asleep nor yet awake
on a brown sagging couch, beneath a length
of gingham curtain neatly taped in place.
He sees white clapboards crying for a coat
of paint, a rotting windowsill, a stack
of bills. A sack of seeds waits for the tractor.

Slipping

Slipping sideways, shallow streams of purple loosestrife
Line the lake edge, water lapping
Where young women, warm and lovely, wade in, willingly yet wary
While young men wait and wonder, yearning to ignore them; eyes
Turned inward, thwarted by their awkward arms and legs, then
Lured to look, like perfect fishes flashing at a summer hook,
Sliding off the shallow courses
Loose between the stream banks
Where their parents' lives have long since stalled,
Strife and passion lost, sideways slipping.

Wandering sorrow

> *Killing is a form of our wandering sorrow...*
> —Rilke, Sonnets to Orpheus, 2.11

Remember Aengus, fresh hazel, berries
ripening like lovers on the green vine.

You have never seen hazel or berries.

Oil from Arabia in barrels
sent to China, plasticized, red as cherries,
slips thin between your soles and burning sand.
You walk toward small ships, bobbing like cherries
in a bucket on a kitchen table.

When the boat sinks in the blue Aegean—
folded paper in a London puddle—
your mother mourns, even as another
soul appears, another voice to reason
that wandering human tides are fungible;
some are better off, and some must suffer.

Shalimar Gardens
Lahore, Pakistan

Nothing is as it seems. This garden of my dreams,
this long-imagined Eden, fabled eponym
of blue-bottled scent of perfumed romance atop
pink-skirted vanities, is crowded wall to wall
with families playing ball under the flickering shade
of ever-present kites boys launch into epic
fights across the sky, dueling desert wings with glass-
encrusted strings, dodging women invisible
behind their fabric gates of black with painted nails
and tattooed marks of beauty that they cannot hide.

You have to pay a man to turn the fountains on.

The water runs, and momentarily the sound
of rushing cool and motion fills the air. Silence
falls and someone lobs a ball again. They tell me
that the person who had paid is transformed by joy,
amazed to feel he brought forth water from dry stone.

A neighbor mows his lawn

Muscled curve of calf descending into
flexing ankle, sneakers worn and battered.
Sweat-soaked grey fleece shorts cut off mid-thigh;
each step reveals a slice of untanned flesh.

A salt-stained triangle of cotton jersey
suspended from the arc of barreled shoulders,
rippling across the small of your back
as you reach the drive, then lean and turn

along my fence-line once again. You brush
away mosquitos, glance up to the sky,
then catch my watching eyes and softly smile,
a gentle nod, a non-committal wave.

The two-stroke hum of Saturdays in August;
a clink of ice cubes, distant thunder rumbles.

The nettle shirt

There is an explanation for evil
and for why the underside of clouds turns
dark with rain and why the storm of pain spills
down, but it lies hidden under tall ferns

by the river's edge, overgrown with sedge
and tendrilled blackthorn roots this time of year.
You're better off walking along the ledge

until the path you're on becomes sincere
and forest dwindles down to farmer's hedge
and seven geese call out that home is near.

The sting of flowering nettles briefly burns
before its fiber yields to flinty knives
and twirls upon the spindle into yarns
that weave the word to answer for our lives.

Blueberries

We are picking blueberries in August
under the raw white sun
inside the hot dry air
inside the cloud of kid complaints and
worries about bears
and when can we go home and
is there any more iced tea.

Your kiss bursts cool and sweet
upon my surprised lips,
and stains my heart forever.

Home garden

Comfrey abuzz with bees, and bishops weed
has overtaken the perennial bed.
Sweet William blooms, and poppies, orange-red,
soldier through tall grass 'round the peony.
Last year's kale boasts thin scraggly flower stalks.
Wild marjoram sprouts in the wood-chip walks.

We've let things go, and I am well aware
of our neighbors' dismay at the sad state
of our affair. The lawnmower won't work
and I stopped looking for my gardening gloves.
They are mistaken if they think we shirk
our duty to restrain nature's estate.
We live, instead, inside a garden where
nothing speaks of love, but everything does.

Depths

In summer's morning light you come to me,
a lithe-limbed dark-eyed boy climbing a hill
through field and beechwood forest, on a trail
that has no end, but runs remembered dreams
of sunlit ridges to the smooth round edges
of my shores; your shirt all buttoned still,
swept upwards in a rush over your head,
pressing shoes off swiftly with your toes,
racing from the pile of tangled clothes
and diving in an aching, arching grin.

Cool water splits and speaks the spells that only
you would know, closing your head over
in the silence of a seamless night,
distant burning yellow day forgotten.
I envelop you in my deep places,
pressing 'till you touch soft, sandy reaches
at the bottom of my soul, your fingers
digging in, as if you seek to stay,
as if you wish to let me
steal your breath away,
and keep you for my own.

Gasping, you burst back into the light,
and full of life, you turn and walk away
while through the winds of all your years and days
I call and call and call again your name,
the ceaseless rippled lapping of my waves.

Blue Mother goes wading

The detritus of our relationship
surrounds me like a plastic continent,
a garbage island in the Atlantic,
a fatally seductive Charybdis.

Look at all this stuff you make me deal with.
Something like a billion head of cattle
and thirty-five billion stupid chickens.
      Sorry chickens, I was rude,
           but that's a lot of chicken shit.

No wonder that the Sapphire Bellied
    hummingbird
    can't breathe
or that the Liliwai just lays her head
    down
      and won't bloom.

I think it's time you stub out that cigar—
think what petroleum does to your lungs—
and shovel out these piles of junked cars.
I started, when the tide was low,
but I could not get far.
When I wade in, I cannot touch the bottom.

Last night

I drank so much. If there had been a pool
or even a fountain, I would have plunged
into it; or a beach, I could have lunged
into the crashing waves.
                                    It was cool
when I was just a kid, to make a fool
out of myself, to do something stupid,
later on to wish I never did it.
But I am old and grey.
                                    Now reason rules,
and rhyme and meter count; now it matters
what other people think, how I'm perceived
and whether I show up to work on time.
I lost my train of thought. My words scatter.
Was there ever a time that I believed
I could hang on to something that was mine.

Photosynthesis
    to Marshall Witten

When things become as hot as this, I can't think straight.
Rain-forest botanists say neither can plant leaves:
When air temp climbs over one-hundred ten degrees
photosynthesis happens at a slower rate.

Less oxygen in our air. Less transpiration
makes the canopy grow hotter still, a spiral
winding down into our DNA, parallel
lines twisting like buckled pavement. Transportation

stalls as planes cannot achieve lift. Food production
drops, commercial crops wiped out by fire, drought or flood.
If I could think, I'd think that none of this is good.

In Times Square, there is a Doomsday Clock that counts down
how close the world comes to nuclear disaster.
They should replace it with a big thermometer.

Turtle of the World

Just when I look down at my iced coffee
the turtle crosses the road. It's as quick
as that. Too late, I lay the brakes on thick.
I hear a thunk, feel it hit all squashy
underneath, then my rear wheels bounce over.
I hear the sharp crack of its hard shell.
Next thing I know, the world has gone to hell.
Coffee spills. I grapple for composure.
Trees fall left and right. Blue sky turns blood red.
People scream and pray. Snakes fill the roadway,
small mice clinging to their backs. Hornets swarm.
Earth rises in a towering black wave,
churning bricks and glass, an end-days storm.
Continents break apart, the planet dead.

I ponder that cool plastic cup, that ice,
coffee and straw, deeply regretting why
I sit here frying in eternal fire:
The turtle of the world had met my tire.

Days of Man

Morning glory and chicory bloom
upon the road abandoned;
blackberry locks the garden gate
where once stood man and woman.
The house is dark, the lane is still,
the chimney, ivy covered.
The Earth reclaims what was taken from her
in fields of crimson clover.
The days of man are over.

A Middle-Aged Woman's Crush in Ten Sonnets

*The face of all the world is changed, I think,
Since first I heard the footsteps of thy soul.*

—Elizabeth Barrett Browning

1: Meeting

You, there, and I wanted needed had to
touch you I had never to this moment
seen you here or anywhere not known
how I had missed absence the shape of you
the gaping empty space I fell into
a gravity so poisonous potent
my lips moved silently swallowed a stone
seething magnetic can't think what to do
engage in small talk staring at the crease
in your white dry-cleaned pique shirt your throat
just begging for the imprint of my teeth
teal conference room carpet swirls afloat
our chairs nearby your thigh pressed mine warm rush—
I had forgotten why they call this 'crush'.

2: The first eight hours

How to write rewrite this nice meeting you
don't send wait no rewrite I enjoyed our
no not our conversing with you an hour
no not time unwind I heard your comment to
no not heard sounds like I am stalking you
and trying not to say the only word
(unsaid) that I am dying to insert
in every (unsaid) line but that won't do
so nice talking to you with you, so nice
perhaps one day soon (unsaid) cup coffee
maybe I can ask your (unsaid) advice

panic panic panic what do I see
in my inbox stare don't click stare twice
yes that must be his name
                                        he messaged me

3: Second meeting

It has been ten days of texts and email
messages and all those early coin-
cidences oh you read that oh you sail
and see you in the morning about ten
then your shape filled the coffeeshop doorframe
barely two minutes late but they were long
minutes to wait impatiently my name
fits neatly on your lips, like it belongs
there but your blue eyes are checking your phone
and mentioning a friend a she a her
touching my hand as you talk such unknown
wondering if I should think this awkward
and now you have to go *the time has flown*
coffee goes cold so fast when I'm alone

4: Feeling foolish

Check text, check phone, check email, whisper *please*
oh please please please please please please please please.
But silence reigns, emptiness, wobbly knees,
a spinning head and stomach filled with dread.

It's foolishness, that, all of it, but good
to know libido still works as it should
even if I grossly misunderstood
everything, infused every word you said

with wishful thinking, foolhardy desire
that wound up setting my self-worth on fire.
I should have known, at my age, to retire
from men and read romance novels instead.

At least I am the only one who knows
unless this foolish sonnet of mine shows.

5: Stasis

I could almost forget this all for hours
at a time. Trees sag and stifling summer sun
sucks all the oxygen out of my lungs.
Yoghurt molds. The half gallon of milk sours.
Brain body spine languish, uncommanded,
curved painfully into a folded chair
that occupies chair-space in heavy air.
I am not waiting. I am suspended,

my spice-market paradigm disrupted.
Objects exist beyond known space.
Such tiny prayers of soft touch were exchanged.

Spores of possibility erupted,
then swirled into the dark abyss of grace.

Attempt to act as if nothing has changed.

6: Diffusion

the distance that a day brings is so in-
teresting, how all that pandemoni-
um can come to nothing, how your phone voice
for an hour held no power whatso-

ever over my breathing or even
worse, there was no curse just distant conver-
sation, no elevated pulse, no con-
sternation, no impulsive confusion.

grey this dismal rain of absolution
grey my skin without a flush of passion
absent grey day-dreams of interaction

when there is no object for affection
no clear glass to hold this dissipation
just a distant flame dimmed by diffusion.

7: Today I deleted your emails

Some days have passed, a couple conversations
by phone but there has been constant rain at home,
dishes and the garden and I feel alone.
Without the flush of desire, my impression
of you changed entirely. My delusion
troubles me; you aren't the man I thought you'd be,
in fact, bit of a jerk if you ask me.
Now I have to parse out my self-deceptions,
figure out why I would fall so hard, so fast
on such thin evidence, light touch of your hand
tapping my wrist, nothing to misunderstand.

Not much mystery, really, why I look past
anything to bring some passion to my life:
the depths of loneliness of an unloved wife.

8: Who am I after this?

The hard clean-up after the storm. The hollow
pit. Flat fields of poison parsnip where golden-
rod and Queen Anne's lace and chicory once grew.
Many hands and many blades and many bits
of dreams blown down; live lines and lost leaves strewn
across roadways. They say the rain went sideways
before it fell, filling wells and river swells
and washing out the unexpected stain. Days
gone by I could not even cry at such scenes,

sunlight illuminating devastation,
irony dripping from forgotten laundry.
Today it all looks brand new. Pink milkweed blooms
and UPS is making deliveries.
Bees on purple hyssop. Wrens on nests. The question.

9: Fly agaric

What is hollowism. What is space between
carmine and alabaster. Ephemeral
gills, frail ribs flaring beneath taut umbrella
skin, piercing dead forest floor with lipstick sheen.

What is obvious. What is it to be seen
spotted and catalogued. Torn and ragged hem
drops away while essence rises on thick stem
and keeps rising. What that up-curled edge might mean

is continuity in motion, spectrum
of states of being, scarlet respite from grey

unrequiting, to witness transition
from self-abhorrence into the damp square vacuum
of an olive woolen blanket where we lay
in unmistakably beautiful poison.

10: Hundred-year storm

I drove right by the barricaded end
of your dirt road before I remembered.
Once upon a time daylight surrendered
to saturated pillars at the bend
of each forward path. I tried to ascend
those dense silver ladders of ablution.
Hard ground gave way and solid rock loosened,
coughed and swallowed mud. Tried to pretend,
like a salesman, that this is something rare.
Call it a hundred-year storm. Violence
that shatters preconceptions, washes out
the yellow smoke and castles in the air.
I drove right by your road in grey silence,
as roads are something I can do without.

Autumn

The autumn days themselves,
Sweet days; so cool, so calm, so bright,
(Yet not so cool either, about noon.)

—Walt Whitman

We needed the rain

soft mists of greyness not enough to saturate the fields
corn aching for the sky
dry, like your fingers reaching for mine then
        never reaching far enough
wrapping ourselves separately, indelibly,
        impermeable against something that might
        fall upon us
        all the more unexpected for our expectations
like jumping when you're waiting for the phone to ring
a fare thee well peck on the cheek, arms
        holding us apart as much or more than
        they might be seen to pull us together
        pushing, not holding
but it looks like an embrace
a heart quenching cloudburst of affection
over fields remaining parched
despite the passing storm.

Culvert

Now everything outside is more extreme.
The dampness and the drought, the flood and fire.
The restlessness at night, the rusted wire
wrapped around the sagging gate. A rough dream
about death. When I woke up, you were gone,
leaving me wrinkled sheets and moldy bread.
A boil-water notice. I must have said,
"I haven't seen the sun in many months"

but my voice sank in the humidity,
stones in the tarmac gap where a culvert
washed away, the heart of the road exposed,
brought to dim light in dank lucidity.
I see what lies beneath is only dirt,
and love is nothing like what I supposed.

A house left empty

A house left empty soon shows signs of decay.
Doors sag, then stick to floors, refusing to close.
Windows seize, each paralyzed in crooked frame.
Plaster flakes, like petals falling from a rose.
A dog, abandoned, trots down empty streets astray,
seeking warm hands, the sound of a voice she knows,
dodging thrown rocks, growling as she's chased away,
dying thin and mangy, picked over by crows.
When crow's feet appear, an unloved wife must choose
whether to fall apart, let face and hair and health
collapse, watch joy drain out, slump down to cold ground;
or take her happiness in her own hands, lose
labels, numbers, rings and things that drain her wealth
of life, buy fresh paint to spread her love around.

Anthropomancy
    outside Gaddani, Pakistan

She is chained
    in the bed
        of a truck
            at the side
        of the road
    to Gaddani.

She is chained
    with a boy
        who is blind,
            hands unlocked
        to shave ice
    for the guests
of the hunters.

    Overhead
        sakar wings
            whisper death
        to the hare
    who will die
in its shade.

    Thin sharp blade
        scrapes the ice
            with the voice
        of a fleet
    whisp of cloud

vanishing
    in white heat
        at midday.
            The girl turns
        her face to
    her brother

in wonder
    of whether
        he glimpses

                        ephemeral
                  visions of
            what would be
      come of them.

Expectation

There is an agony of expectation
of skin that tastes more like the moment before rain
than it does of any familiar thing
like chocolate milk or watermelon.
My fingers trace imaginings of a magnetic
long, thin scar across your back
in rivulets of cold water
running down along a glass of iced tea,
fresh lemon and lightly sweetened.
Tall corn hides your river banks and
willows shade the long, cool lawn of waiting
while I sit in faded plastic chairs,
as patiently displayed as the irises beside the
split rail fence which feigns to be
the boundary of my desire.

Blue Mother has had enough of Progress

You see green; I see invasive knotweed.
Which goes to show that ignorance is bliss.
You'll never have to worry about this:
Everything you worked for in your life, gone to seed,
unrecognizable. Forced to concede
the decades wasted trying to resist
devastation.   So now I reminisce
around the campfire, smoke a little weed
and tell the grandkids how I fought the fight
to keep a piece of this blue planet wild.

You ran the lawnmower over the last
lady slipper. I fainted at the sight
and nearly died then of a broken heart,
while you sulked, *How can I tell them apart?*

Don't you know the face of your own child?

The solid house

Loosely piled high up in an oak's forked limb,
a ragged ball of twigs and last year's leaves
are all the grey squirrel needs to nestle in,
heedless of dark and damp and autumn breeze.
Inside a globe of sheer walls, paper thin,
the wasp withstands the deepest winter freeze,
while hollow trees hide sweet treasure within
the soft warm waxen citadels of bees.
When I saw your silhouette in my door frame
I knew I needed something more substantial—
A slate roof to withstand sleet and driving rain,
walls to block wind, window shutters and wide sills,
doors that could lock out inevitable pain,
if I only knew an architect who had that kind of skill.

Traveler

Rain, when I go about a foreigner,
falls hard and rough, like slate. Unfamiliar.
At home I never use an umbrella
but here I feel the urge for protection,
a roof over my head, a place to hide
while liquid globes of grey pummel my head
and blur the biased vision of my eyes.
Which edifice today dissolved downstream;
which library have I walked by too late,
tangled up in damp sheets and lucid dreams,
eager for *new* but paralyzed by vague
anxiety, of something overdue
to be returned. I know I cannot stay.
Not everyone has streets that wash away.

Gambling

A man wearing a hat stands on the bridge
between Atlantic City and mainland,
one foot in the roadway, one on the edge
of sour miles of salt-channeled marshland
kept apart from ocean by a long ridge
of streets, hotels and houses built on sand.
Cars roll by like dice yet he does not cringe.
He stands his ground, implacable, black hands
winding long thin lines around the wire traps
he'd pulled up from the brine and folded flat,
dropping captured blue crabs into buckets,
claws clacking, grasping at slick white plastic.
A barreling tour bus blows off his hat.
He grabs it, feeling lucky for the catch.

Nature morte

Along the Garden State Parkway
I counted fifteen dead deer,
their spinal columns curled
and rigid, like nautilus shells.

At Mott's Creek, a bald eagle
landed on an osprey platform.
When I looked again, the osprey nest
and fledglings were all gone.

I passed through coastal pines
standing brown and brittle,
ravaged by southern pine beetles,
yearning for a cleansing fire.

A flock of buzzards feasted
on a fresh-killed doe.
Black feathers ruffled as I drove by.
They eyed me coldly, stripping red flesh.

Blue Mother talks with her daughter

Blue Mother, I love your
        autumnal color scheme:
                loosestrife and goldenrod,
                zinnias and marigolds,
                apple red maple leaves,
                sumac in velvet sleeves.

                      Dream daughter, when you were born I looked
                      down on your drunk father's sleeping form.
                      I said, She *looks* like you. That's what I get
                      for head over heels tripping
                      in love with unbridled humanity.

                      Oh, he was so very clever
                      back then,
                      and when I remember how it all began,
                      there are so many things I regret.

                      But that promise, that dream. Oh such dreams,
                      when we met.

Blue Mother, beautiful cradle
    of life, why regret that you have been
    Deep Dreaming's kind mother, and gave
    all of civilization a wife?
            Blue Mother, beautiful
            day is now dawning. Let's
            watch the sun rise and put aside
            sighing.
                    Oh, Mother, why are you crying?

                      Yesterday, I lost another friend
                      and I can feel that my time here
                      is at an end.
                      Daughter Dawn,
                      your life continues on, but I know
                      down in my basalt bones
                      you'll have your own children I'll never see.
                      Your father, that lout,
                      will surely hang on, but it
                      won't be long 'till you forget me.

Climate fire
> *On the loss of Chateau Boswell in the Glass Fire, California 2020*

Charred brown stone. The odor of burnt roses,
red and lingering over desiccated
stems, dead leaves, beauty scarce abated,
even as its essence decomposes,

dissipates into the smoke that poses
as a summer mist, a scene created
as a reverie so long awaited,
castle where a shattered dream reposes.

This is how it is when fire rages
in a nation's soul. Denying facts
kills just as surely as the woodman's axe,

and yet despite the evidence, naught changes.
Perhaps this is the future we have earned,
where castles, vineyards, rose gardens can burn.

Flower and book

> *All these are rested:*
> *darkness and light,*
> *flower and book.*
>   —Rilke, Sonnets to Orpheus, 1.22

The rose unfolds and fades and finally dies.
The book left unfinished sits still and waits,
alive behind the closed lids of mind's eye.
No, now is not the time to speak of fate
or anything at all. Let silence rise.
Surrender your soul over to innate
green wordless spinning earth, deep swelling tide
of night that swelters inside searing day
where light does not dispel long bitter dreams
and dark brings no relief to burning pain.
Each throat aches in memory of water
falling from blue sky in silver streams.
Drought is hollow, brown brittle words explain.
No one recalls the name of the author.

Standing in rain

I have stood in pouring rain, soaked with fear
with sorrow saturating to my core
drenched in everything that I abhor
not blinking as my eyes begin to blear—
wet, yes, wet and cold, with no shelter near
just listening to the thunder gods at war
electric tension filling every pore
with sparkling blue, formed in a perfect sphere.

Catching my death, my mother used to say.
But she is gone, and I still stand in rain
whenever the gods deal out too much pain
for me to bear. I wash my sins away
upon the altar where raw nature reigns,
tattoos my skin, the watermark of Cain.

Winter

*Tonight, this frost will fasten on this mud and us,
Shrivelling many hands, and puckering foreheads crisp.*

—Wilfred Owen

Stick season

Thunder trundles down the valley,
freight-trained November blow,
dumping filled-up cars of frozen rain.
Twigs are thrown on roof and lawn
while limbs cling on to stately trunks
older than anything else that grows
between here and the ridge line.
It's that time. We pile on the clothes
while trees strip to bare sticks. Counter-
intuitive. We burrow while the boles
stand straight and tall, their souls exposed
to cold and wind, then silence once
the snow falls.

Night vision

Firelight. The world is constellated.
Darkness is breached, then seals up seamlessly.
A flash of silver beech bark, pierced cruelly,
tracks of its disease illuminated
between trunk-plates of ancient pine, age-cracked
inside the flickering hegemony
of the visible, the matrimony
between things seen and things perceived as fact.

The forest struggles to remain intact,
crumbling outside the red light of embers.
A limb pops. A shower of sparks rises,
tangles in the canopy, winks out. Stars
all but disappear. Consuming flames flare.
The fragile wisdom of the night contracts.

Love waiting

This is how I found him:

I was living in a blazing day
of summer sun,
a night of ice black winter
frozen over;
watching without wondering,
dreaming on my feet.

I heard the creaking groan of an old
hickory before it fell.

I heard the raucous chorus of
spring peepers in warm mud.

I looked into his eyes.
I said,
he is the one for me.

Silver solstice

Pale sun slides low across the silver sky
and weakly spins a thread of silver light
to hold the force of day against the night,
the all-entombing darkness to defy.
Like mycorrhizal filaments through earth
or water pulsing up through bedrock fault,
light lives, though buried deep within a vault,
like seeds that slumber, dreaming of rebirth.
Silver mist of dawn slips through the oak,
envelops twigs of ash and birch and beech.
Silver tendrils slip and wrap and reach,
bright majesty of morning to uncloak.
      Though darkness wields each facet of its art,
      it cannot tarnish joy within our heart.

Amtrak Ethan Allen Line in February

Between black railroad tracks and roiling grey
mass of winter river, slate-floe coated,
stands an iciclated verge, wild hedge-rowed
bank, bulwark to hold collapsing earth at bay.

Crimson viburnum berries, slender sprays
of alder arched, supplicants devoted
to paths where water rats had passed. Wet-snowed,
while Eastern cedars bowed beneath the glaze.

If the sun was shining, all would glitter,
each fractious beam competing with the next.
But it is dusk, smoke-plum night-dark falling,
barges of churning river ice calling
to encased limbs: Let go. Fall in.
                                       A nest
cups frozen echoes of yellow warblers.

Boundaries

Circling our garden bed, grey fieldstone walls
demarcate the boundary between tall, bright blooms
and mown lawn; yet on velvet green, petals fall
while fescue roots creep under the flowers' rooms.
Framing our snug cottage, four square timber walls
separate warm hearth from winter afternoons,
though open windows bring breezes through our halls
filling the air with rose and balsam perfumes.
But not a single breath can cross the fortress
you construct with pillows, a piled divide
down the center of our bed. No inch of skin
will ever penetrate this wall. Its softness
hides the hardness of the heart kept on your side.
I will surely die before you let me in.

Walnut bowl

The maple table holds a walnut bowl
my father, years ago, had turned by hand
from a downed limb, hit by a lightning bolt
in the near field of his grandparents' land.
The lightning strike gave the farmhouse a jolt,
opened cracks in the foundation that expand
each winter, pathways in for bitter cold.
Things don't always work out the way we planned.
The limb that once shaded our heads now holds
black walnuts we have gathered up by hand,
pulled from branches left on the charred bole.
Inside each gnarled shell a small tree stands,
its trunk erect and sheaves of leaves unfurled
to cradle tiny nests, blossoms to feed
tiny bees. In its roots, the whole wide world
clings to infinite possibility.
It takes firm pressure, lever, hinge and knurl,
to split the two halves apart carefully,
each nut as whole and perfect as a pearl.

Frozen pipes: A love sonnet

Ghostly silent, cold caresses outer walls
of his small house, slips past dove-grey-painted guard
of cedar clapboards, through blue foamboard. It crawls
along dusty baseboards, seeps across waxed hard
wood floors, under closed doors, flows down dim-lit halls.
Inside pipes, water congeals, forms feathered shards
of ice. Copper shudders. Shivering, it calls
for some remembered touch. Warmth. The man is jarred
from warmth of deep, dreamless sleep. His hand reaches
across the vast, empty half of his wide bed
grasping absence as a tightness in his chest.
He tries to rise, swings bare feet down, but freezes,
unafraid, resigned, as his blood vessels burst.
Living on without her would have been far worse.

anxiety (and I become a pearl)

here is slowsteady accretion
layers added to my body
slowform roundpearl of my body
here is round encapsulation

now slowsteady inhalation
count in one two three four hold
count eight move air smooth release hold
now slowsteady exhalation

in the center of the roundpearl
there lies a jagged, broken stone

at the center of my pearlbody
there lies a jagged, broken stone

centered inside my counted breath
lies a sharp stone I cannot hold

Blue Mother sits at her she-shed in Norway, remembering the ice age

northern Norway		nights alone,
dark unending		sky unfurling
silence spinning		stillness staring
watching wild wood	watching, wondering
when the world		was white and wordless

white and wordless
wordless, yes, that wondrous whole
			when winter settled like a blank page

humans were still hunters,
			one of us
			and not yet vermin

			I see an iridescent blue bird
			land on a small twig
			high in a pine.
			Inside the all-day darkness, the twig dips.
			Needles shake.
		no one named things until Adam

life just is
		it feels and flows
it's in the bones
		it's how we know
things, know the things
		themselves and not
the arbitrary

		words are a translation
		like Aristotle moved from Greek to Arabic to Latin
		now there's a Dover Books edition
		but it took a thousand years
		and it was never right

better this silence, in the mind and the inside
		feeling wordlessly in body, in the heart
better being where forgetting, unreminded

A contrail passes overhead.
Even here. Even here.

Closing up the garden, Vermont in December

Warm December rains pour like the River Lethe,
cascading down an angular white trellis
I built with 2X4s and tow-rope lattice,

foreshadow of impending catastrophe.
The trellis height holds delusive enticement
to tropical vines of still-green bottle gourd
wending their defiant, misplaced way skyward
along the clapboard wall. Leaves sketch chastisement

over its lattice grid, obscure words of warning
to us at 45° latitude:

> *No need to close the summer garden up quite yet.*
> *No need to unentwine the vines from their rope lines.*

That trellis frame will withstand global warming.
If I did not know why, I might feel gratitude
for cascading late-season rain; I might forget
that mist is meant to freeze at this point in time.

In the grey light of a winter afternoon

In the grey light of a winter afternoon, I passed away.

The sky between the blue venetian blinds
fell in subdued shadows on my skin.

Your hand, in the stillness of a moment's adoration
rested on the soft white mound of flesh
that held my womb,
then fell through empty space
to touch the hollowed flannel sheets,
smooth and warm to mark the place
my body had been pressed.
Between your startled lips which gasped to catch
the breath of my escaping,
I slipped inside of you, unnoticed;
all that had been my own on earth, separate from you,
had dissipated.

In the grey light of a winter afternoon, I saw myself
dissolved; long-standing ancient stones
in which your aching roots had grown and pulled the earth, the air,
the fire, and the water of your vine. The tiny empty spaces
which the hardest rock encases soon filled to overflowing,
its hidden interstices split
by your pious persistence,
the sweet and perfect passion of your
green sheltering soul.

Into your leaves of words and gentle touch
my wall was drawn;
crumbling in the circle of your arms,
I am gone.

Landscape: Cliffs above the sea

Sometimes the cliff is made of solid rock.
Other times, it crumbles away softly—
grit and shale down-tumbling into the sea,
or fine sand pours off, steady, like a clock.
Sometimes on windy days I see the chalk
dust lifting in a cloud of pearly white,
wet pigments swirled against a slate grey sky.
Each drop of rain encapsulates a rock.

My heart erodes. Time cracked my soul, and ice
has slipped inside. Will it be fast, these last
years of my life, or slow collapse? Sometimes
I want to plant my feet and stand like gneiss,
iconographically, exert a vast
aesthetic influence, paint jagged lines.

Blue Mother writes to Carlo Rovelli about reality

> "The illusion of space and time that continues around us is a blurred vision of this swarming of elementary processes, just as a calm, clear Alpine lake consists in reality of a rapid dance of myriads of miniscule water molecules."
> —Carlo Rovelli, Seven Brief Lessons on Physics, Riverhead Books, 2016, p. 44

Dear Doctor Rovelli,

    In 1992, I saw a boy chained to a loom
in the back room of a shop outside New Delhi.
His iron manacles were in reality
an undiscovered economic field. A single atom
floated freely in a rapid dance
around his ankle, while in gloom
he wove a carpet of silk threads
depicting Alpine wildflower blooms
in brilliant hues of gravity he'd never seen
and would not ever see any time soon.

                              There is no time.
The beautiful blonde at the next table
who you've been watching with Italian eyes
primarily consists of calcium,
and carbon, and some things that she inhaled
from air pollution. The ashes of her body
will seem heavy in her daughter's hands,
though in reality the wind will lift them
one by one, each moment of her life
                              a single, shifting photon.
Leap into my clear turquoise Alpine lake and feel
the water close over the top of your bright
            endothermic cerebellum.
One of my truths will drown you
and another one will wash away your pain.
But there are more truths lurking
        in the depths
        where those two came from.
You can hear them lapping now

        on the far shingled shore:
                particle/wave,

                              particle/wave,

                                            particle/wave.

In reality I am most truly yours,
    —Gaia

Melting (Love in a time of climate change)

Her Valentine box chocolates were melting
melting as she stood there in the red sun
the rose gold sun melting down everyone
drenched in sweat as if it had been raining.
She melted as she read his handwriting
scrawled on the flowered note with a red pen
a pen that flowed red ink like a fountain
fountain of searing sunlight cascading.

In February, ice caps were melting.
        They melted over lovers young and old
            whispering of past days when it got cold
in winter. But these days snows were melting
        practically before they even fell.
        She loved him anyway, though life was hell.

Cindy Ellen Hill published her first poem, about flowers in spring, in 1969 in the Merry Mount Messenger newsletter at her elementary school. She has not stopped writing since, pursuing twin careers in environmental advocacy law and the literary arts including journalism, fiction and poetry.

As a poet, she is primarily a formalist. She has published two chapbooks of sonnets, *Wild Earth* (Antrim Press 2021) and *Elegy for the Trees* (Kelsay Books 2022), and a collection of sonnets, sestinas and terza rima, *Mosaic: Poems and Essays from Travels in Italy* (Wild Dog Press 2024). Her poetry has been included in *Treehouse Literary Review, Flint Hills Review, Anacapa Review, Measure,* and *The Lyric*. She has twice won the Vermont Writer's Prize (formerly the Ralph Nading Hill Award).

She returned to college to complete an MFA in Poetry from VCFA in 2024. Her master's thesis is a historical novel in sonnet verse, *Leeds Point*. She gardens and plays Irish fiddle in Middlebury, Vermont.

www.ingramcontent.com/pod-product-compliance
Lightning Source LLC
Chambersburg PA
CBHW020831190426
43197CB00037B/1534